Classic Cocktails

of the Prohibition Era

100 Classic Cocktail Recipes

Philip Collins

Photography By Sam Sargent

Publisher: W. Quay Hays
Editor: Colby Allerton
Design: Chitra Sekhar

A Fillip Book

Library of Congress Cataloging-in-Publication Data

      Collins, Philip, 1944-
          Classic Cocktails of the Prohibition era / by Philip Collins.
                p.   cm.
          Includes index.
          ISBN 1-57544-020-2
          1. Cocktails. 2. Prohibition—United States. I. Title.
      TX951.C727 1997
      641.8'74—dc21   97-1002
                                               CIP

Drink styling by Andrea Lucich and Dan Becker
Art direction by Philip Collins

For information:
General Publishing Group, Inc.
2701 Ocean Park Boulevard
Santa Monica, California 90405

Printed in Hong Kong through Palace Press International
10 9 8 7 6 5 4 3 2 1

General Publishing Group
Los Angeles

For K.A.T. (again).

CONTENTS:

PROHIBITION

On January 16, 1920, the 18th Amendment, triggered by the Volstead Act, became U.S. law. Prohibition had arrived for an unsuspecting, barely awake public, still reeling from its bold and costly participation in the Great War. Americans woke up to discover they could not drink a drink, purchase a drink, serve a drink or make a drink. Legally. The Drys had won the day and in their view America would be a better place—characterized by an end to drunkenness, a reduction in crime, and a general return to codes of behavior and dress more commonly associated with Victorian England than what was to emerge as the "Roaring Twenties." It was as if the majority in government had been injected with a serum that conditioned them to a blind belief in the tooth fairy.

President Hoover called it a "great social and economic experiment." One thousand five hundred twenty new Federal agents were appointed at an average salary of $1,500 a year to police 18,700 miles of borders and coastline and every state in the union, to keep the country safe from the demon alcohol. It was an open invitation for anyone who was marginally involved in the rackets to enrich themselves beyond their wildest dreams by ensuring an uninterrupted flow of liquor into the country, the country's homes and bars and the speakeasies that emerged on every city block (an estimated 100,000 in New York City alone).

Bootlegging from Canada, ship-to-shore transfers in powerful speedboats, illicit stills in backyards and cellars, hundreds of ships anchored off the 3-mile limit (later to be 12 miles, to no effect whatever) kept "dry" America wetter than it had ever been. Cash payoffs down the line to the lowliest cop on the beat, up through all branches of law enforcement and legislature, became commonplace. A still, operating on the farm of Morris Sheppard, was discovered to be turning out 130 gallons of whiskey a day. Sheppard was the senator who authored the 18th Amendment. Home brewing became the most popular hobby for thirsty citizens, operating simple distilling apparatus, built from kits available at any hardware store, and set up in the nation's basements, bathrooms, closets and outhouses. A popular poem read:

"Mother makes brandy from cherries;
Pop distills whiskey and gin;
Sister sells wine from the grapes on our vine—
Good grief how the money rolls in!"

A vast organization of undercover liquor distribution, driven in trucks from the stills of farmers and covert import depots at the docks to the back doors of speakeasies and bars of upscale residences, blossomed in cities and small towns across the country. Internecine warfare determined who controlled major territories in Chicago, Detroit, New York and Philadelphia. The most influential (and coincidentally the most brutal) mobster to emerge as bootlegging kingpin was Alphonse Capone. Known as "Scarface" to both friends and enemies, he redefined the term "friendship," often blurring the usual connotation so that it ended in a hail of bullets, a river of blood and a lavish funeral for the "friend." The new tactics were universally adopted among the denizens of organized crime. Machine Gun Jack McGurn, William Klondike O'Donnell, Polack Jack Saltis, Little Hymie Weiss, Johnny Torrio, Big Jim Colisimo and George Bugs Moran all fought the good fight, mostly ending up under huge garlands of flowers en route to their premature, final resting places.

At the height of this reign, Capone was estimated to be grossing $60 million a year before payoffs. Running liquor to his own speakeasies (either owned or "protected"), Capone catered to a young generation of potential hedonists whose flirtations with the "daring" of haunting the illicit niteries were about as dangerous as TP-ing the Headmaster's lawn. The younger generation, however, had more than illicit booze to fuel their social revolution. As girls' hemlines went north, their morals and attitudes traveled south, mainly in the back of newly mass-produced automobiles that impacted the social mores of the young with a greater influence than any bottle of illicit hooch.

The Jazz Age, providing new syncopated rhythms, new mobility and access via the car, rocketing popularity of motion pictures and radio and the rise of magazine publishing with such titles as *True Story* witnessed a liberation of social behavior for women as significant as any decade in the twentieth century. A motion picture publicized as "brilliant men, beautiful jazz babies, champagne baths, midnight revels, petting parties in the purple dawn, all ending in one terrific smashing climax that makes you gasp!" pretty well sums it up. Once inside the speakeasy, having given the password at the door, revelers were able to enjoy any cocktail that was available prior to Prohibition, plus a few that weren't. With an inconsistency of quality in some of the basic liquors (gin, whiskey, brandy) came imaginative concoctions to improve and smooth away the rougher edges of less refined spirits. Popular among the additional ingredients were grenadine, bitters, absinthe (now no longer considered healthy for today's refined palates), Anisette and the juices of limes, lemons and oranges.

With names like Shady Lady, Fine and Dandy, Knock-Out, Vanderbildt, Thunderbird, Pink Rose and Fallen Angel, it's easy to see why the romance and excitement of the Cocktail era is enjoying a new surge of popularity.

After 14 years of adventures in the gin trade, the government under FDR repealed Prohibition on December 5, 1933. The "great social experiment" was finally over. A monumental folly that tried to enforce the unenforceable, gave rise to organized crime and branded half the nation as felons went quietly into the night with a faint splash, which sounded curiously like a Bronx cheer.

INTRODUCTION

Mixing a drink is not an exact science. It is a social accommodation that should be simple, pleasurable and ultimately satisfying for the consumer. H. L. Mencken hired a mathematician to discover the number of cocktails that could be mixed from the ingredients of an average, well-stocked bar. The total was 17,864,392,788. Of these he sampled 273 "at random" and "found them all good." One hundred examples are recommended here. Whether any were tasted by Mencken, we shall never know, but the range of tastes is broad and anyone who enjoys whiskey, gin or brandy should find a cocktail from the Prohibition era to delight the palate.

A basic stock for any bar will include gin, whiskey, brandy, rye, and light and dark rum. Mixers should include sweet and dry vermouth, Anisette, crème de menthe, ginger ale, club soda, grenadine and bitters. Fresh fruit—oranges, lemons and limes—are preferred to preserved juices. Basic mixing hardware includes a shaker (preferably metal or stainless steel), a strainer, a jigger for measuring, a long stirring spoon, olive spears and a sharp knife.

Crucial to the experience is a supply of cracked ice that should be replaced after every pouring. (The ice will melt if left in the shaker and dilute the next cocktail to an unpalatable degree.) Cracked ice is simply cubes from the deep freeze that have been hammered into smaller pieces.

Some simple guidelines will enhance the pleasure and ensure the success of your cocktails:

~ Don't guess measurement. Use a jigger. After a few mixes, your taste will determine the "right" amount for you and the balance may be altered to personal preference. Use the best brand-name liquor you can afford.
~ Use fresh ice every time.
~ When mixing drinks containing fruit juices or sweeteners, pour the spirits last.
~ Use only fresh juice as mixers, never canned or frozen.
~ Don't use juices that have been refrigerated for more than 24 hours.
~ For sweetening, powdered sugar is recommended over other types and substitutes.
~ It is important to follow directions: Shake means shake—a vigorous motion is employed, not a rocking to and fro. Stirring should be done without vigor. Shaking creates a cloudy drink; stirring makes it clear.
~ Don't allow a cocktail to stand too long. It should be enjoyed as soon as possible after mixing.
~ Never use "ready-made" cocktails or mixed drinks from cans or "mix" bottles.
~ Use the best glass and stemware you can afford. With care, a lifetime of pleasure can be enjoyed by serving drinks in beautiful glasses. Glassware products from the companies featured in the following illustrations can only enhance the enjoyment of a drink. A selection of martini, old-fashioned, collins, wine, and champagne glasses will accommodate 90 percent of cocktails.

"When I sell liquor, it's bootlegging. When my patrons serve it on Lakeshore Drive, it's hospitality."

Alphonse Capone

FINE AND DANDY
COCKTAIL

~ Juice of $1/4$ lemon

~ $1/2$ ounce Triple Sec

~ $1 1/2$ ounces gin

~ 1 dash bitters

Shake with ice and strain into cocktail glass. Serve with a cherry.

Fine And Dandy Cocktail/Orrefors Wolfie Martini Glass

SHADY LADY

~ 1 ounce tequila

~ 1 ounce melon liqueur

~ 4 ounces grapefruit juice

Combine ingredients in highball glass over ice. Garnish with a lime and a cherry.

Shady Lady/Baccarat Monaco Highball Glass

POOP DECK COCKTAIL

~ 1 ounce brandy

~ 1 ounce port

~ 1 tablespoon blackberry-flavored brandy

Shake with ice and strain into cocktail glass.

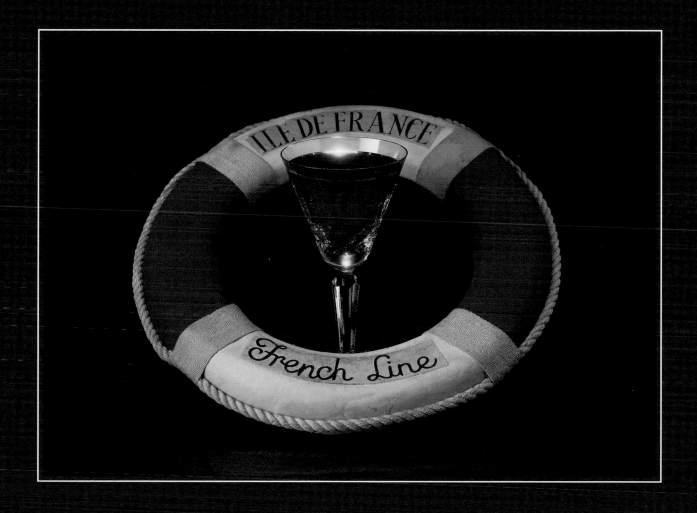

Poop Deck Cocktail/Waterford Maeve Claret Glass

KNOCK-OUT COCKTAIL

- ~ $^1/_2$ ounce Anisette

- ~ $^3/_4$ ounce gin

- ~ $^1/_4$ ounce dry vermouth

- ~ 1 teaspoon white crème de menthe

Stir with ice and strain into cocktail glass. Serve with a cherry.

Classic Cocktails

Knock-Out Cocktail/Saint Louis Grand Lieu Burgundy #3 Glass

GIN & SIN

~ 1 ounce gin

~ 1 ounce lemon juice

~ 1 tablespoon orange juice

~ 1 dash grenadine

Shake with ice and strain into cocktail glass.

Gin & Sin/Tharaud Designs Chantilly White Wine #2 Glass

SNOWBALL

~ 1$\frac{1}{2}$ ounces gin

~ $\frac{1}{2}$ ounce Anisette

~ 1 tablespoon light cream

Shake with ice and strain into cocktail glass.

Classic Cocktails

Snowball/Baccarat Massena White Wine #4 Glass

PINK LADY COCKTAIL

- ~ The white of 1 egg

- ~ 1 tablespoon grenadine

- ~ 1$^{1}/_{2}$ ounces pink gin

Shake well with ice and strain into medium-sized glass. Decorate with mint.

Pink Lady Cocktail/Waterford Curraghmore Old-Fashioned Glass

KIR ROYALE

~ 6 ounces chilled champagne

~ 1 splash crème de cassis

Serve in large champagne flute or white wine glass.

Classic Cocktails

Kir Royale/Moser Royal Champagne Flute

MAH-JONGG COCKTAIL

~ 1 teaspoon Cointreau

~ 1 teaspoon Bacardi rum

~ $1\frac{1}{2}$ ounces dry gin

Shake well with ice and strain into cocktail glass. Decorate with a lemon slice.

Mah-Jongg Cocktail/Gumps Bamboo Martini Glass

PORT WINE SANGAREE

- ~ $^1/_2$ teaspoon powdered sugar

- ~ 1 teaspoon water

- ~ 2 ounces port

- ~ Club soda

- ~ 1 tablespoon brandy

Dissolve sugar in water in highball glass. Add port and ice cubes. Fill with club soda to near top of glass and stir. Float brandy on top and sprinkle with nutmeg.

Classic Cocktails

Port Wine Sangaree/Baccarat Capri/Montaigne Optic Tumbler #2

SHAMROCK

~ 1 1/2 ounces Irish whiskey

~ 1/2 ounce dry vermouth

~ 1 teaspoon green crème de menthe

Stir with ice and strain into cocktail glass. Serve with an olive.

Classic Cocktails

Shamrock/Hoya Brezza Red Wine Glass

CHARLIE CHAPLIN

~ 1 ounce sloe gin

~ 1 ounce apricot brandy

~ 1 ounce lemon juice

Shake with ice and strain into cordial glass.

Classic Cocktails

Charlie Chaplin/Saint Louis Bristol Sherry #5 Glass

SILK STOCKINGS

~ 1$\frac{1}{2}$ ounces tequila

~ 1 ounce crème de cacao

~ 1$\frac{1}{2}$ ounces cream

~ 1 dash grenadine

Shake ingredients with crushed ice, and strain into large cocktail glass. Sprinkle cinnamon on top.

Classic Cocktails

Silk Stockings/Baccarat Perfection Martini Glass

BISHOP

~ juice of $1/4$ lemon

~ juice of $1/4$ orange

~ 1 teaspoon powdered sugar

~ Burgundy

Shake with ice and strain into highball glass. Add two ice cubes, fill with burgundy and stir well. Decorate with fruits.

Classic Cocktails

Bishop/Waterford Lismore 12-Ounce Tumbler

HOT BUTTERED RUM

~ 1 teaspoon brown sugar

~ Boiling water

~ 1 tablespoon butter

~ 2 ounces dark rum

Put sugar into punch cup and fill two-thirds full with boiling water. Add butter and rum. Stir and sprinkle nutmeg on top.

Hot Buttered Rum

GRAND ROYAL FIZZ

~ Juice of $1/2$ orange

~ Juice of $1/2$ lemon

~ 1 teaspoon powdered sugar

~ 2 ounces gin

~ $1/2$ teaspoon Maraschino liqueur

~ 2 teaspoons light cream

~ Club soda

Shake with ice and strain into highball glass over two ice cubes. Fill with club soda and stir.

Classic Cocktails

Grand Royal Fizz/Cristal de Sevres Corinthe Double Old-Fashioned Tumbler

TIPPERARY COCKTAIL

~ $^3/_4$ ounce Irish whiskey

~ $^3/_4$ ounce green Chartreuse

~ $^3/_4$ ounce sweet vermouth

Stir with ice and strain into cocktail glass.

Tipperary Cocktail/Waterford Carleton Gold Martini Glass

UNCLE SAM SPECIAL

~ $1/4$ ounce brandy

~ $1/4$ ounce gin

~ $1/4$ ounce dry vermouth

~ $1/4$ teaspoon lemon juice

Shake with ice and strain into cocktail glass. Serve with a cherry.

Classic Cocktails

Uncle Sam Special/Moser Ophelia Red Wine Glass

DEPTH BOMB

~ 1 ounce apple brandy

~ 1 ounce brandy

~ 1 dash lemon juice

~ 1 dash grenadine

Shake with ice and strain into old-fashioned glass over ice cubes. Serve with straws.

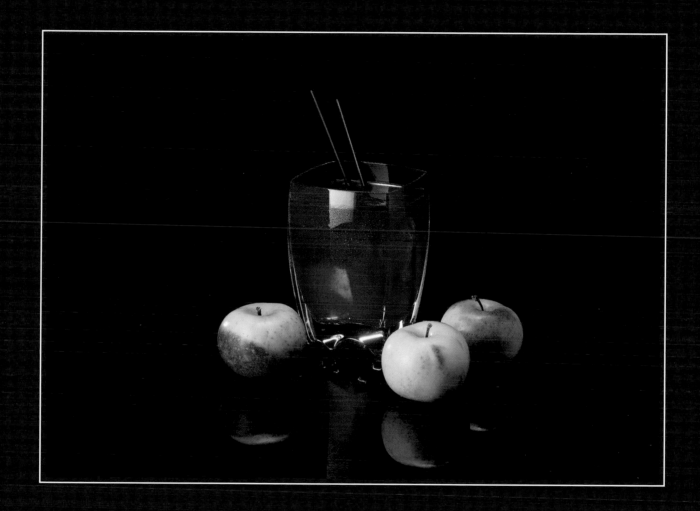

Depth Bomb/Baccarat Oceanie Glass

EVERYBODY'S IRISH COCKTAIL

~ 1 teaspoon green crème de menthe

~ 1 teaspoon green Chartreuse

~ 2 ounces Irish whiskey

Stir with ice and strain into cocktail glass. Serve with a green olive.

Everybody's Irish Cocktail/Baccarat Capri Red Wine #3 Glass

BASIN STREET

~ 2 ounces bourbon

~ 1 ounce Triple Sec

~ 1 ounce lemon juice

Shake well with cracked ice and strain into cocktail glass.

Basin Street/Riedel Sommeliers Martini Glass

HORSE'S NECK

~ 2 ounces blended whiskey

~ Ginger ale

Peel rind of whole lemon in spiral fashion and place in collins (tall) glass with one end hanging over rim. Fill glass with ice cubes and add blended whiskey. Fill with ginger ale and stir well.

Classic Cocktails

Horse's Neck/Iittala Aarne Pilsner Glass

CHINESE COCKTAIL

~ 1 tablespoon grenadine

~ 1 1/2 ounces Jamaican rum

~ 1 dash bitters

~ 1 teaspoon Maraschino liqueur

~ 1 teaspoon Triple Sec

Shake with ice and strain into cocktail glass.

Chinese Cocktail/Baccarat Vienne Gold Saucer Champagne Glass

FRISCO SOUR

~ Juice of $^1/_4$ lemon

~ Juice of $^1/_2$ lime

~ $^1/_2$ ounce Bénédictine brandy

~ 2 ounces blended whiskey

Shake with ice and strain into sour glass. Decorate with slices of lemon and lime.

Frisco Sour/Baccarat Ligne Double Old-Fashioned Glass

SCOTCH ROYALE

~ 1 cube sugar

~ 1$\frac{1}{2}$ ounces Scotch whiskey

~ 1 dash bitters

~ Chilled champagne

Place sugar cube in champagne flute. Add Scotch and bitters. Fill with champagne.

Classic Cocktails

Scotch Royale/Baccarat Orsay Champagne Flute

FRENCH 75

- ~ Juice of 1 lemon

- ~ 2 teaspoons powdered sugar

- ~ 2 ounces gin

- ~ Chilled champagne

Stir in collins (tall) glass. Add ice cubes, fill with champagne and stir. Decorate with a slice of lemon or orange and a cherry. Serve with straws.

French 75/Block Trinidad Highball Glass

MARY PICKFORD COCKTAIL

~ 1 ounce light rum

~ 1 ounce pineapple juice

~ $\frac{1}{4}$ teaspoon grenadine

~ $\frac{1}{4}$ teaspoon Maraschino liqueur

Shake with ice and strain into cocktail glass.

Mary Pickford Cocktail/Waterford Golden Lismore Tall Wine Glass

TEQUILA HIGHBALL

~ 1 $^1\!/_2$ ounces tequila

~ Slice of lemon

~ Ginger ale

Pour tequila over two ice cubes into a highball glass. Fill with ginger ale. Add lemon slice.

Tequila Highball/Baccarat Monaco #2 Double Old-Fashioned Glass

SMILER COCKTAIL

~ 1 dash Angostura bitters

~ 1 dash orange juice

~ $\frac{1}{2}$ ounce Italian vermouth

~ $\frac{1}{2}$ ounce French vermouth

~ 1 ounce dry gin

Shake well with ice and strain into cocktail glass.

Smiler Cocktail/Baccarat Vega Martini Glass

ROB ROY

~ $^3/_4$ ounce sweet vermouth

~ $1^1/_2$ ounces Scotch whiskey

Stir with ice and strain into cocktail glass.

Rob Roy/Saint Louis Cerdagne Burgundy #3 Glass

SILVER BULLET

~ 1 ounce kümmel

~ 1 ounce gin

~ 1 tablespoon lemon juice

Shake with ice and strain into cocktail glass.

Silver Bullet/Orrefors Nobel Martini Glass

T.N.T. Cocktail

~ 1 ounce Canadian whiskey

~ 1 ounce absinthe

Shake well and strain into cocktail glass.

T.N.T. Cocktail/Saint Louis Provence #3 Burgundy Glass

CLARET COBBLER

~ 1 teaspoon powdered sugar

~ 2 ounces club soda

~ 3 ounces claret

Dissolve powdered sugar in club soda and then add claret. Fill red wine glass with ice and stir. Decorate with fruits in season. Serve with straws.

Claret Cobbler/Saint Louis Tommy #3 Burgundy Glass

MAIDEN'S PRAYER

- ~ 1$\frac{1}{2}$ ounces gin
- ~ $\frac{1}{4}$ ounce dry vermouth
- ~ 1 ounce lemon juice

Shake with ice and strain into cocktail glass. Add twist of lemon.

Maiden's Prayer/Baccarat Oxygene Red Wine #3 Glass

THUNDERBIRD

~ 1$\frac{1}{8}$ ounces Canadian whiskey

~ $\frac{3}{4}$ ounce Amaretto

~ 2 ounces pineapple juice

~ 1 ounce orange juice

~ 2 dashes grenadine

Shake with ice and strain into highball glass filled with ice. Garnish with an orange slice and a cherry. Serve with a straw.

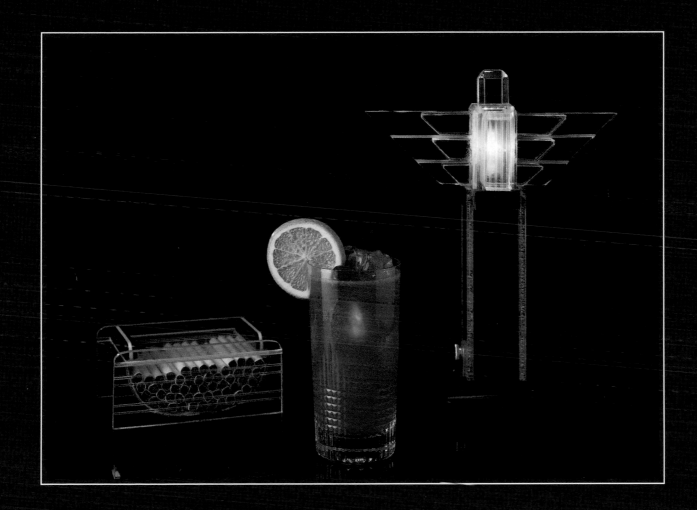

Thunderbird/Baccarat Nancy Highball Glass

PINK ROSE COCKTAIL

~ The white of 1 egg

~ 1 teaspoon grenadine

~ 1 teaspoon lemon juice

~ 1 teaspoon sweet cream

~ $1^{1}/_{2}$ ounces dry gin

Shake well with ice and strain into cocktail glass.

Pink Rose Cocktail/Hoya Spring Crocus Red Wine Glass

UNION JACK COCKTAIL

~ $^3/_4$ ounce sloe gin

~ $1^1/_2$ ounces gin

~ $^1/_2$ teaspoon grenadine

Shake with ice and strain into cocktail glass.

Union Jack Cocktail/Gumps Charisma Cocktail Glass

WHISKEY SWIZZLE

- ~ Juice of 1 lime
- ~ 1 teaspoon powdered sugar
- ~ 2 ounces club soda
- ~ 2 dashes bitters
- ~ 2 ounces blended whiskey

Put lime juice, sugar and soda into large-stemmed glass. Fill glass with ice and stir. Add bitters and whiskey. Top up soda and serve with a swizzle stick.

Whiskey Swizzle/Baccarat Lyra #2 Water Goblet

SOMBRERO

~ 1 $^1/_2$ ounces coffee-flavored brandy

~ 1 ounce light cream

Pour brandy into old-fashioned glass over ice cubes. Float cream on top.

Sombrero/Baccarat Triade #2 Double Old-Fashioned Glass

FALLEN ANGEL

- Juice of 1 lime or $^1/_2$ lemon

- $1^1/_2$ ounces gin

- 1 dash bitters

- $^1/_4$ teaspoon Triple Sec

- $^1/_4$ teaspoon powdered sugar

Shake with ice and strain into cocktail glass. Add a twist of lemon peel.

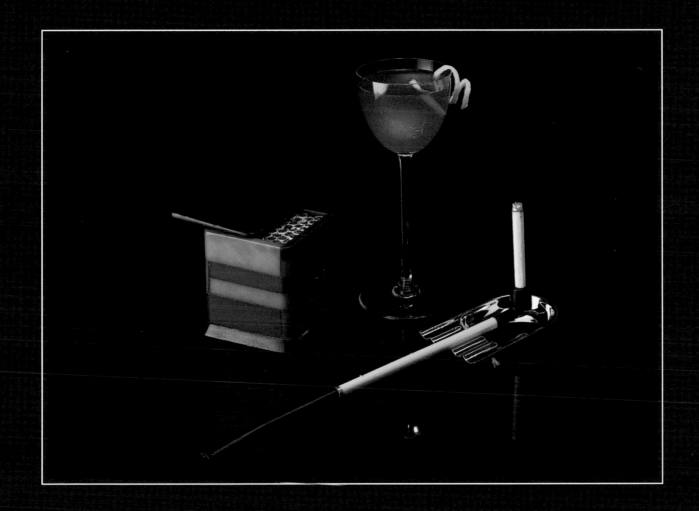

Fallen Angel/Baccarat Montaigne Rhine Wine Glass

FLYING DUTCHMAN

~ 2 ounces gin

~ 1 dash Triple Sec

Shake with ice and strain into old-fashioned glass over ice cubes. Decorate with lemon rind.

Flying Dutchman/Baccarat Nancy Tumbler #2

BRANDY GUMP COCKTAIL

~ 1 $^1/_2$ ounces Brandy

~ Juice of $^1/_2$ lemon

~ $^1/_2$ teaspoon grenadine

Shake with ice and strain into cocktail glass. Add muddler.

Brandy Gump Cocktail/Baccarat Nancy Saucer Champagne Glass

ROBERT E. LEE COOLER

~ Juice of $^1/_2$ lime

~ $^1/_2$ teaspoon powdered sugar

~ 2 ounces club soda

~ $^1/_4$ teaspoon Anisette

~ 2 ounces gin

~ Ginger ale

Pour first three ingredients in collins (tall) glass. Stir. Add ice cubes, Anisette and gin. Fill with ginger ale and stir again. Add a spiral of orange or lemon peel (or both) and dangle end over rim. Serve with a straw.

Classic Cocktails

Robert E. Lee Cooler/Waterford Marquis Hanover Gold Highball Glass

CLOVER CLUB COCKTAIL

~ $\frac{1}{2}$ ounce grenadine

~ The white of 1 egg

~ 2 ounces gin

Shake well with ice and strain into medium-sized glass. Decorate with fruit.

Clover Club Cocktail/Cristal de Sevres Mila Tumbler

FOGHORN

~ Juice of $^1/_2$ lime

~ 1 $^1/_2$ ounces gin

~ Ginger ale

Pour into highball glass over ice cubes. Fill with ginger ale. Stir. Add a slice of lime.

Foghorn/Baccarat Harmonie Tumbler #2

WIDOW'S KISS

~ 1 ounce brandy

~ $^1/_2$ ounce yellow Chartreuse

~ $^1/_2$ ounce Bénédictine brandy

~ 1 dash bitters

Shake with ice and strain into cocktail glass.

Widow's Kiss/Kosta Boda Epoque Gold Claret Glass

ROLLS ROYCE

~ $\frac{1}{2}$ ounce dry vermouth

~ $\frac{1}{2}$ ounce sweet vermouth

~ $1\frac{1}{2}$ ounces gin

~ $\frac{1}{4}$ teaspoon Bénédictine brandy

Stir with ice and strain into cocktail glass.

Classic Cocktails

Rolls Royce/Saint Louis Bubbles Martini Glass

CAFE DE PARIS COCKTAIL

~ The white of 1 egg

~ 3 dashes Anisette

~ 1 teaspoon fresh cream

~ $2\frac{1}{2}$ ounces gin

Shake well with ice and strain into medium-sized glass. Serve with a straw.

Cafe de Paris Cocktail/Iittala Stella 9-Ounce Juice Glass

VANDERBILDT COCKTAIL

~ $^3/_4$ ounce cherry brandy

~ $1^1/_2$ ounces brandy

~ 1 teaspoon simple syrup

~ 2 dashes bitters

Stir with ice and strain into cocktail glass.

Vanderbildt Cocktail/Saint Louis Apollo Gold Martini Glass

IRISH COFFEE

~ 1 $\frac{1}{2}$ ounces Irish whiskey

~ Hot coffee

Rim Irish coffee glass with sugar. Pour in Irish whiskey. Fill to ½ inch from rim with coffee. Cover surface to brim with whipped cream.

Classic Cocktails

Irish Coffee

BRAZIL COCKTAIL

~ 1¹/₂ ounces dry vermouth
~ 1¹/₂ ounces dry sherry
~ 1 dash bitters
~ ¹/₄ teaspoon Anisette

Stir with ice and strain into cocktail glass.

ABSINTHE SPECIAL COCKTAIL

~ 1¹/₂ ounces Anisette
~ 1 ounce water
~ ¹/₄ teaspoon powdered sugar
~ 1 dash orange bitters

Shake well and strain into cocktail glass.

BULL AND BEAR

~ 1¹/₂ ounces bourbon
~ ³/₄ ounce orange Curaçao
~ 1 tablespoon grenadine
~ Juice of ¹/₂ lime

Shake with cracked ice and strain into cocktail glass. Garnish with a cherry and orange slice.

CALIFORNIA LEMONADE

~ Juice of 1 lemon
~ Juice of 1 lime
~ 1 tablespoon powdered sugar
~ 2 ounces blended whiskey
~ ¹/₄ teaspoon grenadine
~ Club soda

Shake well and strain into collins (tall) glass over shaved ice. Fill with club soda and decorate with orange and lemon slices. Add a cherry. Serve with straws.

BLARNEY STONE COCKTAIL

~ 2 ounces Irish whiskey
~ ¹/₂ teaspoon Anisette
~ ¹/₂ teaspoon Triple Sec
~ ¹/₄ teaspoon Maraschino liqueur
~ 1 dash bitters

Shake well and strain into cocktail glass. Add a twist of orange peel and an olive.

CABLEGRAM

~ Juice of ¹/₂ lemon
~ 1 teaspoon powdered sugar
~ 2 ounces blended whiskey
~ Ginger ale

Stir with ice cubes in highball glass and fill with ginger ale.

CANAL STREET DAISY

~ Juice of ¹/₄ lemon
~ Juice of ¹/₄ orange
~ 1 ounce blended whiskey
~ Club soda

Pour all ingredients into collins (tall) glass over ice cubes. Add club soda and an orange slice.

CHARLES COCKTAIL

~ 1¹/₂ ounces sweet vermouth
~ 1¹/₂ ounces brandy
~ 1 dash bitters

Stir with ice and strain into cocktail glass.

DERBY DAIQUIRI

~ 1¹/₂ ounces light rum
~ 1 ounce orange juice
~ 1 tablespoon lime juice
~ 1 teaspoon sugar

Shake well with shaved ice and strain into champagne flute.

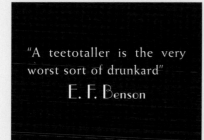

"A teetotaller is the very worst sort of drunkard"
E. F. Benson

DIPLOMAT

~ 1¹/₂ ounces dry vermouth
~ ¹/₂ ounce sweet vermouth
~ 2 dashes bitters
~ ¹/₂ teaspoon Maraschino liqueur

Stir with ice and strain into cocktail glass. Serve with half slice of lemon and a cherry.

EAST INDIA COCKTAIL #2

~ 1¹/₂ ounces dry vermouth
~ 1¹/₂ ounces dry sherry
~ 1 dash orange bitters

Stir with ice and strain into cocktail glass.

GENE TUNNEY COCKTAIL

~ 1 dash orange juice
~ 1 dash lemon juice
~ ¹/₂ ounce french vermouth (white)
~ 1¹/₂ ounces dry gin

Shake well and strain into cocktail glass.

GENTLEMAN'S COCKTAIL

~ 1¹/₂ ounces bourbon
~ ¹/₂ ounce brandy
~ ¹/₂ ounce crème de menthe
   club soda

Pour bourbon, brandy and creme de menthe over ice into highball glass. Add club soda and garnish with lemon twist.

HARVARD COCKTAIL

~ 1¹/₂ ounces brandy
~ ¹/₄ ounce sweet vermouth
~ 1 dash bitters
~ 1 teaspoon grenadine
~ 2 teaspoons lemon juice

Shake well and strain into cocktail glass.

HIGHLAND FLING COCKTAIL

~ ³/₄ ounce sweet vermouth
~ 1¹/₂ ounces Scotch whiskey
~ 2 dashes orange bitters

Stir with ice and strain into cocktail glass. Serve with an olive.

HONEYMOON COCKTAIL

~ ³/₄ ounce Bénédictine brandy
~ ³/₄ ounce apple brandy
~ Juice of ¹/₂ lemon
~ 1 teaspoon Triple Sec

Shake well and strain into cocktail glass.

HOT CINNAMON ROLL

~ 1¹/₂ ounces cinnamon schnapps
~ Hot apple cider

Pour hot cider into Irish coffee glass. Add schnapps. Top with whipped cream and add cinnamon stick as stirrer.

HURRICANE

~ 1 ounce dark rum
~ 1 ounce light rum
~ 1 tablespoon passion fruit syrup
~ 2 teaspoons lime juice

Shake well and strain into cocktail glass.

IDEAL COCKTAIL

~ 1 ounce dry vermouth
~ 1 ounce gin
~ ¹/₄ teaspoon Maraschino liqueur
~ ¹/₂ teaspoon grapefruit juice

Shake well and strain into cocktail glass. Serve with a cherry.

JOCKEY CLUB COCKTAIL

~ 1 dash bitters
~ ¹/₄ teaspoon white crème de cacao
~ Juice of ¹/₄ lemon
~ 1¹/₂ ounces gin

Shake well and strain into cocktail glass.

KENTUCKY BLIZZARD

~ 1¹/₂ ounces bourbon
~ 1¹/₂ ounces cranberry juice
~ ¹/₂ ounce lime juice
~ ¹/₂ ounce grenadine
~ 1 teaspoon sugar

Shake with cracked ice and strain into old-fashioned glass half-filled with cracked ice. Garnish with ¹/₂ orange slice.

KISS-IN-THE-DARK

~ ³/₄ ounce gin
~ ³/₄ ounce cherry brandy
~ ³/₄ ounce dry vermouth

Stir with ice and strain into cocktail glass.

LEAP FROG HIGHBALL

~ Juice of ¹/₂ lemon
~ 2 ounces gin
~ Ginger ale

Pour into highball glass over ice cubes and fill with ginger ale. Stir.

LITTLE DEVIL COCKTAIL

~ Juice of ¹/₄ lemon
~ 1¹/₂ teaspoons Triple Sec
~ ³/₄ ounce light rum
~ ³/₄ ounce gin

Shake well and strain into cocktail glass.

LOUISVILLE LADY

~ 1 ounce bourbon
~ ³/₄ ounce white crème de cacao
~ ³/₄ ounce cream

Shake with ice and strain into cocktail glass.

114

MODERN COCKTAIL

~ 1 1/2 ounces Scotch whiskey
~ 1/2 teaspoon lemon juice
~ 1/4 teaspoon Anisette
~ 1/2 teaspoon Jamaican rum
~ 1 dash orange bitters

Shake well and strain into cocktail glass. Serve with a cherry.

LOUNGE LIZARD

~ 1 ounce dark rum
~ 1/2 ounce Amaretto
~ Cola

Pour rum and Amaretto into ice-filled collins (tall) glass. Fill with cola. Garnish with a slice of lime.

MAMIE GILROY

~ Juice of 1/2 lime
~ 2 ounces Scotch whiskey
~ Ginger ale

Combine in collins (tall) glass with ice. Fill with ginger ale and stir.

MIAMI

~ 1 1/2 ounces light rum
~ 1/2 ounce white crème de menthe
~ 1 dash lemon juice

Shake well and strain into cocktail glass.

MONTMARTRE COCKTAIL

~ 1 1/4 ounces dry gin
~ 1/2 ounce sweet vermouth
~ 1/2 ounce Triple Sec

Stir with ice and strain into cocktail glass. Serve with a cherry.

MOULIN ROUGE

~ 1 1/2 ounces sloe gin
~ 3/4 ounce sweet vermouth
~ 1 dash bitters

Stir with ice and strain into cocktail glass.

57 EAST 54TH STREET

MUrray hill 2 | 8744
8040

NIGHT CAP

~ 2 ounces light rum
~ 1 teaspoon powdered sugar
~ Warm milk

Pour rum and sugar in Irish coffee glass. Fill with warm milk and stir. Sprinkle nutmeg on surface.

NIGHTMARE

~ 1 1/2 ounces gin
~ 1/2 ounce Madeira
~ 1/2 ounce cherry brandy
~ 1 teaspoon orange juice

Shake well and strain into cocktail glass.

ORANGE BLOSSOM

- ~ 1 ounce gin
- ~ 1 ounce orange juice
- ~ 1/4 teaspoon powdered sugar

Shake well and strain into cocktail glass.

PALM BEACH COCKTAIL

- ~ 1 1/2 ounces gin
- ~ 1 1/2 teaspoons sweet vermouth
- ~ 1 1/2 teaspoons grapefruit juice

Shake well and strain into cocktail glass.

POPPY COCKTAIL

- ~ 3/4 ounce white crème de cacao
- ~ 1 1/2 ounces gin

Shake well and strain into cocktail glass.

PREAKNESS COCKTAIL

- ~ 3/4 ounce sweet vermouth
- ~ 1 1/2 ounces blended whiskey
- ~ 1 dash bitters
- ~ 1/2 teaspoon Bénédictine brandy

Stir with ice and strain into cocktail glass. Add a twist of lemon peel.

PRINCETON COCKTAIL

- ~ 1 ounce gin
- ~ 1 ounce dry vermouth
- ~ Juice of 1/2 lime

Stir with ice and strain into cocktail glass.

RORY O'MORE

- ~ 3/4 ounce sweet vermouth
- ~ 1 1/2 ounces Irish whiskey
- ~ 1 dash orange bitters

Stir with ice and strain into cocktail glass.

PERROQUET
134 EAST 61st STREET
NEW YORK CITY

RUM SWIZZLE

- ~ Juice of 1 lime
- ~ 1 teaspoon powdered sugar
- ~ 2 ounces club soda
- ~ 2 dashes bitters
- ~ 2 ounces light or dark rum

Pour lime juice, sugar and 2 ounces club soda into collins glass. Fill with ice and stir. Add bitters and rum. Fill with club soda and serve with swizzle stick.

RYE WHISKEY COCKTAIL

- ~ 1 dash bitters
- ~ 1 teaspoon powdered sugar
- ~ 2 ounces rye whiskey

Shake well and strain into cocktail glass. Serve with a cherry.

SAXON COCKTAIL

- ~ Juice of 1/2 lime
- ~ 1/2 teaspoon grenadine
- ~ 1 1/4 ounces light rum

Shake well and strain into cocktail glass. Serve with a twist of orange.

SCOOTER

~ 1 ounce Amaretto
~ 1 ounce brandy
~ 1 ounce light cream

Shake well and strain into cordial glass.

SCOTCH STINGER

~ $^1/_2$ ounce white crème de menthe
~ 1$^1/_2$ ounces Scotch whiskey

Shake well and strain into cocktail glass.

SENSATION COCKTAIL

~ Juice of $^1/_4$ lemon
~ 1$^1/_2$ ounces gin
~ 1 teaspoon Maraschino liqueur

Shake well and strain into cocktail glass. Add sprigs of mint.

"I exercise extreme self-control. I never drink anything stronger than gin before breakfast."
W. C. Fields

"I drink when I have occasion, and sometimes when I have no occasion."
Miguel de Cervantes

ST. GERMAIN COCKTAIL

~ Juice of $^1/_2$ lemon
~ Juice of $^1/_4$ grapefruit
~ The white of 1 egg
~ 1 liqueur glass green Chartreuse

Shake well and strain into cocktail glass.

STAR COCKTAIL

~ 1 ounce apple brandy
~ 1 ounce sweet vermouth
~ 1 dash bitters

Stir with ice and strain into cocktail glass.

SUN KISS

~ 2 ounces Amaretto
~ 4 ounces orange juice

Combine in collins (tall) glass filled with ice. Garnish with a wedge of lime.

TULIP COCKTAIL

~ 1$^1/_2$ teaspoons lemon juice
~ 1$^1/_2$ teaspoons apricot brandy
~ $^3/_4$ ounce sweet vermouth
~ $^3/_4$ ounce apple brandy

Shake well and strain into cocktail glass.

WARD EIGHT

~ Juice of $^1/_2$ lemon
~ 1 teaspoon powdered sugar
~ 1 teaspoon grenadine
~ 2 ounces blended whiskey

Shake well and strain into large glass filled with cracked ice. Add slices of orange and lemon and a cherry. Serve with straws.

"I am omnibibulous. I drink every known drink and enjoy them all."
H. L. Mencken

117

All the Classic
Cocktails were mixed
according to the
prescribed recipes by
Steve Zell at the bar
of The Cypress Club,
San Francisco.